Lord, Teach Us To Push!

Pray Until Something Happens!

Bishop Carrie J. Surratt

Printed in the US
Published by Harrod Publishing LLC

Lord, Teach Us To Push!
Pray Until Something Happens!
Bishop Carrie J. Surratt   ISBN 978-0-9997275-8-4

TABLE OF CONTENT

DEDICATION

ACKNOWLEDGEMENTS

FOREWORD

INTRODUCTION

CHAPTER ONE	Prayer Is	1
CHAPTER TWO	Assignment To Pray	12
CHAPTER THREE	Prayer Potentialities	24
CHAPTER FOUR	Declare /Decree … Praying The Word – Part I	35
CHAPTER FIVE	"WORD Hit" … Praying The Word - Part II	44
CHAPTER SIX	When We Pray	54
CHAPTER SEVEN	Biblical Praying Men And Women	67
CHAPTER EIGHT	Jesus, The Teacher Of Prayer	79
END NOTES		89
AFTERWORD		90
BIOGRAPHY		94

DEDICATION

I humbly dedicate this book to two "Prayer Warriors" who shaped my life of holiness and my prayer life by the example of their own lives; and by the love they both demonstrated for the Lord. Pastor Vivian Iren Posey of Arlington, Virginia and Mother Inez Hall of Salisbury, North Carolina, who now rest in glory, were instrumental in my spiritual foundation and development during my teenage years; and I am so grateful. Their guidance and inspiration will forever be remembered.

Also, I dedicate this book to my household family members, especially my daughter Tina who always understood my purpose for being in my room in front of the computer writing, instead of being in the kitchen cooking. I am excited about the completion of this book, because now you can read what I have lived and practiced before you for years. I love each of you dearly and thank you for supporting me.

ACKNOWLEDGMENTS

My sincere thanks and first acknowledgment is for ArchBishop Ralph L. Dennis, who wrote the foreword. I am thankful for his instructions, his mentorship, and his tremendous encouragement. I deeply appreciate him trusting me to oversee the prayer ministry of Kingdom Fellowship Covenant Ministries for years. Considering our prayer ministry relationship, ArchBishop Dennis was the best individual to craft the foreword for this book on prayer. Thank you Sir!

I am forever grateful to my writing coach, Professor Latonia-Valincia Moss, who has extensive educational accomplishments and successful teaching skills. Thank you for the many mid-day telephone calls, the late-night sessions on Zoom and the many hours of giving me instructions and praying for me. You are a true inspiration to me and I look forward to our coach/student relationship for my next three books.

I want to acknowledge my membership crew at The Lord's Church of Restoration who always encouraged me to write so they could buy my books. Especially my chief cheerleader Minister Verta Larkins, who consistently checked on my writing status; and Elder Merry Jones, Elder Shari Hubbard, and Mother Patricia Baker, my prayer warriors who prayed me through birthing pains and delivery of the book. I am thankful for your tremendous prayer support, which helped me successfully complete this writing project.

Finally, I wish to acknowledge my daughter Tina for assisting me with technical issues and writing advice while tolerating moments of frustration. You always solved the problems or taught me how to correct them with great patience. I love you and deeply appreciate your love and support.

FOREWORD

After calling his readers to pray in times of trouble and sickness and to confess their sins one to another, James asserts the following, "...*The effective prayer of a righteous man can accomplish much*" (James 5:16). To illustrate effective and powerful prayer, James then refers to the prophet Elijah as an example of a person who had a powerful and effective prayer life. James tells us that Elijah's prayers both began and ended a three-and-a-half-year drought on the nation of Israel (see 1 Kings 17 and 18). James also reminds us that Elijah was a man with a nature just like us (James 5:17). In other words, he [Elijah] had no superhuman powers; he was by nature, a human being and nothing more. However, when he prayed 'that it would not rain ... it did not rain' (cf. 1 Ki 17:1-18:42-45)...so James assures his readers that such answers to prayer are within the reach of any believer.

If it is true that we can have a powerful and effective prayer life like the prophet Elijah, then the obvious question is, "How?" Many books propose answers to this question by suggesting we do things such as recite a verse or a word repeatedly, sit in silence (an altered state of consciousness), or walk a prayer circle. Prayer, however, is not some magical incantation or manipulative tool we can use to control God. As Jesus Himself taught, "*And when you are praying, do not use meaningless repetitions as the Gentiles do, for they suppose that they will be heard for their many words*" (Matthew 6:7). Instead, prayer is communicating with God through means by which He has revealed in His word.

Recognizing that we are dependent upon the Bible to understand prayer, Carrie Surratt presents prayer as a birthing process in her book LORD, TEACH US TO PUSH! - Pray Until Something Happens. After defining prayer, she shares with her readers the potentialities of prayer and the necessity of prayer being understood as an assignment in every believer's life.

One of the most impactful thoughts for me in having a powerful and effective prayer life is to model our prayer life after Jesus Christ. Jesus' life was defined by prayer. At the start of his ministry, as He was baptized, He prayed (Luke 3:21). Before He chose His disciples, He spent time in prayer (Luke 6:12-16).

Before He was betrayed, arrested, and condemned to death, He was on His knees in prayer (Matthew 26:36; Mark 14:32; Luke 22:41; John 17). The display of this consistent pattern of prayer obviously left an impression on Jesus' disciples as we find them asking Jesus, when He was finished praying, just how to pray. *"It happened that while Jesus was praying in a certain place, after He had finished, one of His disciples said to Him, 'Lord teach us to pray just as John also taught his disciples'"* (Luke 11:1). While it was common at this time for rabbis to compose prayers for their disciples, the question by the disciples was more than just wanting to have a prayer to recite. They had already been taught by Jesus how prayer was not a showy presentation (Matthew 6:5) nor just the reciting of words (Matthew 6:7). Instead, I believe they wanted the same power and effectiveness Jesus demonstrated in His prayer life. The disciples had been used to going to the synagogues and the temple and hearing the cold, impersonal, repetitious prayers of the Pharisees. But once they began following Jesus, they must have immediately noticed that His prayer life was different. It was passionate and powerful. It was much different than what they were used to. When Jesus prayed, things happened. Jesus' prayer life commanded the disciples' attention enough for them to ask Him for instruction on how to pray.

As we look to model our prayer lives after Jesus, just like the disciples did, this book will inspire you to pray with the expectation of getting results. Carrie calls it "pray(ing) until something happens (PUSH)!" This is praying with the confidence, assurance and resources needed to get results, evidence, and change.

I have known Carrie Surratt for almost forty years. Prayer has long been the trademark of her spiritual life. She models prayer and teaches others how to strategically pray. Please, take time to read it, perhaps, again and again until the strategies of prayer produce long-lasting evidences in your life. Get more than one copy and sow a copy into the life of a family member or friend. Believe me, they will be eternally grateful. LORD, TEACH ME TO PUSH… is a must read and should be a part of your library. Be blessed as you read it.

Your Kingdom Servant,

++ *Ralph L. Dennis*

Presiding Prelate, Kingdom Fellowship Covenant Ministries

INTRODUCTION

At the age of twelve, I had a prophetic prayer encounter with the Lord while visiting my cousins in Lexington, North Carolina. What I heard, saw and felt left an indelible mark in my spirit, a desire to have a relationship and connection with the Lord who answers the prayer as I had witnessed. Two years later, at age fourteen, the preacher preached the Word and offered prayer for those who wanted and needed to be saved and WOW! I experienced the Presence of the Lord and realized I had encountered His Presence two years earlier. My life was forever changed through prayer.

I believe the day I accepted Jesus as Lord and Savior, and the desire to pray was birthed within me; however, I knew very little about the real essence of prayer, even though I had heard and seen individuals pray and apparently receive answers to their prayers. My questions within were: What is prayer? How do I pray? Will God hear me? If God hears me, how will He answer? What do I say to get God to answer? The first two or three years after I was saved, I had an insatiable thirst to pray to God and to pray for others; therein, I started my quest to learn all I could about prayer.

I learned a lot about prayer from my first pastor, who was known as a praying pastor with a deliverance ministry. She taught me many facets of prayer, and I activated what I learned by offering to pray for family, friends, and neighbors. Educationally, I studied at George Washington University, taking all the religious courses available to me; then, I completed my studies at Washington Bible College and Rhema Bible School. My life pursuit has been to know all I can about God, to understand His Word, improve my relationship with Him, study various facets of prayer, and spend time in His Presence.

One of my deepest heart's desires and prayers has been for the Lord to position me to educate, train, and equip others about prayer. I have conducted many leadership seminars and workshops, revivals, retreats, and special day services, wherein prayer is ALWAYS one of the main focuses because of the desire and need of the attendees. The door has opened for me to fulfill my heart's desire concerning prayer thus, I am writing this book, "Lord, Teach Us to PUSH – Prayer Until Something Happens!

+ *Carrie J. Surratt*

CHAPTER 1

"Prayer Is"

Prayer? What is it? Prayer is conversation, communication, and communion with God. Prayer is the powerful and effective vehicle by which we relate to God, our needs, desires, wants and concerns. The word "prayer" comes from the Latin word *precare,* which means to beg, ask earnestly. *"The earnest (heartfelt, continued) prayer of a righteous man makes tremendous power available – dynamic in its working"* James 5:16b (Amplified Bible). The Greek word for pray is *proseuchomai* and was used in the New Testament 90 times. The meaning is to want, desire, or wish toward. There are a number of synonyms for the word prayer, and the following are a few from the list:

petition, supplication, request, appeal, implore, intercede and beseech. Combining the definitions from the Latin and the Greek words, I define the nature of prayer is to ask, plead and/or request.

By definition, prayer is a devout petition to God. It is a conversation with God and spiritual communion with Him. Prayer is a supplication, with thanksgiving, adoration and/or confession. Also, by definition, prayer is a religious observance, either public or private, a petition or an entreaty.

It is imperative that we communicate with our Heavenly Father constantly and consistently through supplications, implorations, appeals, and petitions. We do this in confidence and in accordance to what the Word says I John 5: 14, 15 (NLT): *"And we can be confident that he will listen to us whenever we ask him for anything in line with his will. And if we know he is listening when we make our requests, we can be sure that he will give us what we ask for."* Our Father is a good father who will answer his children when we pray.

Prayer is a conversation between man and God, it is a dialogue, which means an exchange of ideas and opinions. A conversation is the interchange of thoughts and information through spoken words. It is oral communication. We talk with God sharing our thoughts and desires, and God responds sharing His heart with us. According to the law of first mention, it has been taught that the first prayer was in Genesis 3: 8-13, when Adam and Eve hid themselves as God walked into the garden. This was actually the first dialogue recorded in Scripture between God and man. Just know when you talk to God, He will respond. The account of the second prayer in the Bible is in Genesis 4: 26, which says after the birth of Seth's son: *"At that time, the men began to call [upon God] by the name of the Lord."* (Amplified)

It is essential for us to communicate with our Father because communication is a vital necessity in a valid relationship. God is our Father and we are His children, we should communicate with Him regularly, daily and throughout the day. A genuine and authentic relationship is developed with open communication. According to the dictionary, communication is the imparting or interchange of thoughts, opinions or information by speech, writing, or signs. Also, by definition, communication means something imparted, interchanged or transmitted. Consequently, prayer communication is the imparting or interchanging of thoughts unto God by speech or written petition. Talk with the Father in prayer, dialog with Him daily and allow time for thoughts, desires, and intentions to be shared in prayerful communication.

Prayer is communication with God! Communicating with God opens heaven and makes available to us all of the power in heaven for our earthly situations. Prayer is the most proactive and effective thing you can do. According to James 5:16b in the New Living Translation: *"The earnest prayer of a righteous person has great power and produces wonderful results.* I remember when there was communication between earth and heaven on my behalf when I needed a miracle. The prayer warriors talked to God and communicated through prayer my needs and my requests.

Prayerful communication of Samson gave him access to the power of heaven in his last prayer. His prayer was short yet precise in Judges 16:28: *"Then Samson called to the LORD and said, "O Lord GOD, please remember me and please strengthen me just this one time, O God, and let me take vengeance on the Philistines for my two eyes."* There was communication between earth and heaven, Samson prayed to God in heaven, God heard his prayer and answered him. Samson knew he was facing death –his death and the death of the enemy. We must always pray confidently and with faith, knowing that God will hear and answer our prayer regardless of the situation we are facing.

David provides excellent examples of prayer as communication with thanksgiving between earth and heaven in Psalms 61:1-3(Amplified): *"Hear my cry, O God; Listen to my prayer. From the end of the earth I call to You, when my heart is overwhelmed and weak; Lead me to the rock that is higher than I [a rock that is too high to reach without Your help]. For You have been a shelter and a refuge for me, A strong tower against the enemy."* David cried out to God, and his deliverance was God answering his prayer. If you read Psalm 61 in its entirety, you will note there is praise, adoration and thanksgiving which are all part of David's prayer.

Thankful communication should be included in our dialogue with God. Another perfect example in Scripture is Psalm 63:1-4 (Amplified) when David was in the wilderness of Judah: *"O God, You are my God; with deepest longing I will seek You; My [a]soul [my life, my very self] thirsts for You, my flesh longs and sighs for You, In a dry and weary land where there is no water. So I have gazed upon You in the sanctuary, To see Your power and Your glory. Because Your lovingkindness is better than life, My lips shall praise You. So will I bless You as long as I live; I will lift up my hands in Your name."* David offered his supplication and requests to the Lord, and then began to bless, praise and glorify His name. It is favorable to give praise and thanksgiving when communicating with God in prayer. The Bible tells us in everything, by prayer and petition, with thanksgiving present our requests to the Lord. Gladly offer your petitions, supplications and intercessions to the Lord with a thankful heart.

Moses spent quality time with Jehovah God in conversational prayer. Surely forty days would be considered quality time. Let us take an inside glimpse of Moses, who was the chosen deliverer for the Israelites; and he brought them out, he brought them over and he brought them across. Moses brought the Israelites out of Egyptian bondage and the Wilderness; and he brought them over many hills, mountains and tough terrain. In addition, he brought them across the dry ground of the Red Sea by following the directions and instructions of Jehovah God. Moreover, Moses was a remarkable intercessor, who bridged the gap between God and the Israelites, in as much as he conversed, fellowshipped, communicated, and communed with God face to face.

Moses alone was invited to draw near to God for a one-of-a-kind "mountain top" experience of quality time, which lasted forty days and nights. Moses prayed to God, he dialogued, communicated, communed, and fellowshipped with Jehovah. The following account in Exodus 33: 14-20 (NIV) is a perfect demonstration of prayer as a dialogue wherein Moses talked, and God answered.

> *14 The LORD replied, "My Presence will go with you, and I will give you rest."*
> *15 Then Moses said to him, "If your Presence does not go with us, do not send us up from here.*
> *16 How will anyone know that you are pleased with me and with your people unless you go with us? What else will distinguish me and your people from all the other people on the face of the earth?"*
> *17 And the LORD said to Moses, "I will do the very thing you have asked, because I am pleased with you and I know you by name."*
> *18 Then Moses said, "Now show me your glory."*
> *19 And the LORD said, "I will cause all my goodness to pass in front of you, and I will proclaim my name, the LORD, in your presence. I will have mercy on whom I will have mercy, and I will have compassion on whom I will have compassion. 20 But, he said, "You cannot see my face, for no one may see me and live."*

Prayer is a dialogue – you talk, God listens; God talks, and you listen. Moses had a conversation with the Almighty God. Absolutely, prayer is not a monologue, wherein you do all the asking or speaking. A dialogue is a conversation between two or more persons. God and Moses conversed! They communicated and fellowshipped during the mountain top experience of forty days.

Prayer is spiritual communion and fellowship also. When you apply the words communion and fellowship to prayer, they identify several things: 1) relationship and intimacy; 2) harmony and togetherness; 3) the interchange or sharing of thoughts and/or emotions; and 4) mutuality and solidarity. Furthermore, prayer is an intimate exchange of deep and sincere thoughts of thanksgiving, communication, supplication or confession; and it is also the opportunity to share emotions. I believe prayer is significant to God, and He desires to hear from His children. There is a standing invitation to come boldly and to draw near to Him. Our relationship with the Father is enhanced when we commune and fellowship with Him. It is during this time of prayer; God will reveal His heart to you. Prayer always takes us to God, it summons His Presence, and He responds to us. Prayer opens the gateway for effective communication between God and His creation. Prayer is the vehicle by which our relationship with God becomes intimate, close and heart-felt. Spiritual communion and fellowship, which is prayer, affords us the opportunity to demonstrate our dependence on Him and our faith in His promises.

Spending time in the Presence of the Lord is very beneficial as it enhances the relationship. I encourage you to long to know God! To know in Hebrew means intercourse, an intimate exchange of thoughts and expressions. The Scriptures tells us in Jeremiah 24:7, that God will give us a heart to know Him and we shall be his people. In Hosea 6:3a it says: *"Let us know; let us press on to know the Lord..."* Quality prayer time in His Presence positions us to intercourse with Him, exchange intimate thoughts and share heart issues. That is powerful!

It is essential for your communication skills to be shaped by faith as you engage in a dialogue with the Lord or have a prayer conversation with Him. When you begin praying, hallow (which means to make holy or sanctify) the name of God, esteem Him, revere Him, and adore Him. Communicate to God earnestly your requests and anticipate God answering your prayers. Remember, prayer is a dialogue! Wait on the Lord confidently! He will respond, He will answer. In Genesis 38:10, God answered Jacob in the day of his distress and God was with him. Also, Job communicated and conversed with God about his life, he prayed. God answered and responded to Job (Job 38:1, 40:1, 2, and 42:10). God answers prayer!

We must pray, entreating earnestly and consistently, as Daniel did. Even in the face of adversity and threats, Daniel prayed three times a day, he knew His God would hear and answer his prayers and petitions. God heard the prayers, God answered, and God delivered Daniel. All throughout the New Testament are examples of God answering prayer. We believe unequivocally that the prayers of the righteous are powerful and effective. The Bible says if we pray according to His will, He hears us and if He hears us, we are confident He will respond or reply. God answers prayer!

CHAPTER 2

"Assignment To Pray"

QUESTIONS:

Is prayer the assignment of intercessors and prayer warriors only?

Could prayer be the sole responsibility of the "prayer team"?

According to the Scriptures, it is the assignment and responsibility of everyone to pray. In Luke 18:1(NCV) it says: *"Then Jesus used this story to teach his followers that they should always pray and never lose hope."* Everyone is required to call on the name of the Lord, to pray without ceasing, to be constant in prayer and to beseech the Lord confidently in prayer. It does not matter what your title or position is, ALL Believers, Christians, Children of the Most High, Intercessors, Prayer Band Members, Prayer Warriors and members of the Body of Christ are required to pray. Everyone is admonished in the Word to pray: pray without ceasing; pray for one another; and to pray according to the will and word of the Lord.

The first mention and example of prayer in the Bible is in Genesis 4: 26, which says: *"Seth also had a son, and he named him Enoch. At that time men began to call on the name of the Lord."* This passage refers to the establishment of regular public instances where men began to address God formally in worship, prayer, and thanksgiving. The first notable prayer occurs when Abraham pleads with God not to destroy the people of Sodom. According to the Hebrew Bible, organized prayer was introduced in Deuteronomy when Moses mandated and established the liturgy to be recited when offering the fruit sacrifice. Everyone, from leaders like Moses, Aaron, Joseph, Jacob, Joshua, Deborah, Samuel, as well as the people prayed.

There is a universal call and need to pray according to Psalms 65:2 & 5, which says we make vows to God, and He answers our prayers. We must offer prayer. We must ask by praying and then God answers. That Scripture goes on to say God faithfully answers our prayers with awesome deeds. Pray to God with expectancy because He is the only God who hears and answers prayer; therefore, after praying, we must expect His answer to come. The Bible also says: *"These I will bring to my holy mountain and give them joy in my house of prayer. Their burnt offerings and sacrifices will be accepted on my altar; for my house will be called a house of prayer for all nations."* Isaiah 56: 7(NIV)

This universal mandate to pray is an assignment to ALL.... Bishops, Apostles, Prophets, Evangelists, Pastors, Teachers, Elders, Deacons, Ministers, Inner Ministry Workers, as well as to believing members of the Body of Christ. Unfortunately, prayerlessness has found a seat in the lives of too many leaders in the house of the Lord. God's house is to be a house of prayer, led by praying men and women. It is significant to fulfill the assignment to pray, not just to get answers, but to improve our relationship with God through prayerful communication. Individuals, especially those in leadership, should follow the many examples found in the Scriptures of leaders having an authentic and valid relationship with the Lord through a viable prayer life. In Scripture, there are many examples of leaders praying for direction, guidance, to know God, pray for the sick to be healed, and for deliverance from the enemy. A partial list of examples will be addressed in chapter 4.

It is unfortunate that the responsibility to pray has been shifted again to prayer groups, prayer teams, and intercessory groups, wherein leaders have decreased their time in prayer, having become too busy and too involved in developing strategies to grow the ministry.

WARNING: Do not fall prey to the "sin of prayerlessness!"

Prayerlessness causes disconnection, insensitivity, and apathy! We must be watchful and guard against prayerlessness in our personal lives, in our churches, or in our ministries. Prayer must remain a foundational and spiritual focus to accomplish the work the Lord has placed in our hands to do. Prayer must be and remain the most important element of ministry. Why? Because prayer enhances our relationship with God, it is our line of communication and fellowship. Prayer is a spiritual weapon against warfare, and it is the most powerful and proactive activity we can do. There is no place for "prayerlessness" if we obey the Word that says men should always pray and if we willingly accept our assignment to pray one for another. We will avoid prayerlessness if we continually offer supplications and petitions to God and practice praying persistently to God, who always answers prayer.

When I think about the prayerlessness in leadership today, it saddens my heart. I wonder how it makes God feel when his "open door prayer policy" is ignored by prayerlessness. All leaders with any measure of authority must pray. Let us review what I refer to as "God's open-door prayer policy" in the book of Hebrews. In fact, we will look at it in three different translations below:

1)   Hebrews 4:16(KJV)

> *"Let us, therefore, come boldly unto the throne of grace that we may obtain mercy, and find grace to help in time of need."*

2)   Hebrews 4:16 (NCV)

> *"Let us, then, feel very sure that we can come before God's throne where there is grace. There we can receive mercy and grace to help us when we need it."*

3)　　　Hebrews 4:16 (AMP)

"Let us then fearlessly and confidently and boldly draw near to the throne of grace (the throne of God's unmerited favor to us sinners), that we may receive mercy [for our failures] and find grace to help in good time for every need [appropriate help and well-timed help, coming just when we need it]."

God has an open-door prayer policy! Everyone, regardless of title, position, or gender must simply approach the throne of grace boldly and persistently in prayer. The open-door policy also includes an invitation to pray secretly. In Matthew 6:6 (Amplified) says: *"But when you pray, go into your most private room, close the door and pray to your Father who is in secret, and your Father who sees [what is done] in secret will reward you."* We have access to our Father God through consistent, persistent, or secret prayer. If we pray according to the Scriptures, we will avoid the pit of prayerlessness. In Luke 18:1, Jesus said to his disciples that they should always pray and not give up. And in the same Scripture in the Amplified Bible, it says we ought always to pray and not turn coward; we are not to faint, lose heart or give up. We must keep praying!

The Passion Translation of I Thessalonian 5:17 states the verse is personally instructive, and it says: *"Make your life a prayer"*. Yes, you pray when you get up, pray as you go throughout the day, pray, pray, pray! The New Living Translation of I Thessalonians 5:16-18 encourages us even further: *"Always be joyful. Keep on praying. No matter what happens, always be thankful, for this is God's will for you who belong to Christ Jesus."* Persistent communication with the Lord is indispensable and imperative, regardless of what is happening in or around your life. It is our assignment to pray; so be encouraged and keep on praying!

The Scriptures encourage, counsel, enlighten and instruct us regarding our prayer assignment. Read Ephesians 6:18 below in two different translations of Scripture:

Ephesians 6:18 New International Version

> *"And pray in the Spirit on all occasions with all kinds of prayers and requests. With this in mind, be alert and always keep on praying for all the Lord's people."*

Ephesians 6:18 New Living Translation

"Pray in the Spirit at all times and on every occasion. Stay alert and be persistent in your prayers for all believers everywhere."

I must reiterate the necessity for everyone, including those in authority and leadership, to have an active, personal prayer life. There must be personal time of communication, communion, and fellowship with the Lord; wherein, directions, instructions, steps of guidance, and yes, even corrections will be received. Consequently, spending quality time with God in prayer, practicing the discipline of solitude, interceding, travailing or praying in the Spirit for hours will defeat prayerlessness in our lives. The Bible says it like this: *"Pray at all times (on every occasion, in every season) in the Spirit, with all [manner of] prayer and entreaty. To that end, keep alert and watch with strong purpose and perseverance, interceding on behalf of all the saints (God's consecrated people)."* (Ephesians 6:18 Amplified)

It is imperative, especially as a leader in the Body of Christ, that we take the helm and steer the way of prayer to those who are our spiritual responsibility. Our prayers must be offered consistently and persistently to confidently ensure that there is dialogue between earth and heaven.

Relationships, in general, are strengthened by consistent conversation and dialogue. The reality of developing a closer relationship with the Lord is consistent conversation and dialogue by prayer and supplication. It is noteworthy to follow the instructions and example in Matthew 7:7-11, regarding persistent prayer. Verse 9 says: *"So I say to you: Ask and it will be given to you; seek ad you will find; knock and the door will be opened to you." (NIV)*

THE LESSONS – instructs us to A.S.K. – ask, seek and knock. In asking, request or inquire of the Father and He will respond. We make our petitions known and God answers. The Bible says everyone who asks will receive. It also says in the Passion Bible, verse 8a *"For every persistent one will get what he asks for."* We make our requests and petitions known by persistently asking, and God will answer.

When we seek, we inquire of Him and He will show us great and mighty things. Seeking is a deeper form of asking, wherein, we explore, or analyze or investigate to know. We are instructed in the Scripture that if we seek God, inquiring for and requiring Him as our first need, our Lord will answer.

Knocking is a repeating motion and a persistent action to open or gain access. When we knock, the door will be opened and a way will be made. When we knock, we get God's attention and He responds with answers and opens the way for opportunities. Persistent prayer to our Father will enhance our relationship and will give us answers to our requests and grant us access to the blessings He has for us.

We will eliminate the "sin of prayerlessness" by the practice of this lesson on persistent praying. In practicing the "A.S.K." principle, our relationship is strengthened as we receive answers, as doors are opened and ways are made for us. Also, we find ourselves praying more confidently as we ask, seek and knock, because we know God to be a good, good Father who will hear and answer our humble cry.

It is the assignment of everyone to pray because prayer is one of the primary forces in the lives of believers. Each person, regardless of a leadership title or spiritual calling, has the responsibility and assignment to offer to God prayers, supplications, and petitions. Prayers are submitted from a heart of love and profound reverence for God who is love and He is sufficient in power to answer our requests.

God is sovereign, He is all-powerful and faithful to His word. The responsibility to offer petitions, supplications and requests to God is ours. We have been instructed to abide in the Lord and allow His Word to abide in us, then whatever we ask will be done for us. We must pray! The Bible addresses calling on the Lord and receiving answers in Jeremiah 33:3 (ESV). It says: *"Call to me and I will answer you and will tell you great and hidden things that you have not known."* Further, the Bible says: *"Therefore I tell you, whatever you ask in prayer, believe that you have received it, and it will be yours."* (Mark 11:24 ESV) Willingly accept the assignment to pray, to communicate with God, to pray His Word and His will. Keep on praying, God answers prayer!

CHAPTER 3

"Prayer Potentialities"

Prayer is vitally important as it is our communication, communion, and conversation with God. Prayer is a gift from God filled with potential, possibilities, promise, and power. The reach of prayer is enormous, spanning into all areas of life, accomplishing purposes, and delivering unusual results. Prayer reaches whatever God's plans are for us and whatever His purposes are for us. The Bible says in John 14:13 (NAS) "Whatever you ask in My name, that will I do, so my Father may be glorified in the Son." The reach of prayer summons grace, which is sufficient for us and peace that passes all understanding as we receive answers to our requests.

After I read in Ephesians 3:18 concerning the breadth, height and depth of God's love, I had an epiphany. The breadth, height and depth of prayer defines the reach of prayer, which penetrates all things and expands over and into all areas of life. Our understanding the potentiality of prayer's reach will assist us in praying more confidently in faith regardless of the difficulty of the prayer concern. A word-filled prayer, declaration, decree or proclamation has sufficient power to seek out and deliver answers. God watches over His word to perform it and He is the power that will bring it to fruition.

The potential of prayer is astronomic and massive. So much so, until mans' finite mind has some difficulty grasping hold of its intensity and effectiveness. Prayer, a supernatural gift of power, allows us to communicate directly to God, who is all-powerful, allows us to seek His face, and allows us to prayerfully worship the Creator of all things. In James 1:5, it says if we lack wisdom, we are to ask in prayer, and it will be given. Also, in Jeremiah 33:3(ESV) it says: *"Call to me and I will answer you and will tell you great and hidden things that you have not known."*

Prayer activates and energizes the reaching force of prayer which is power; power to heal body, soul and spirit, miracle-working power and power to deliver. In

Psalms 77: 14 (NIV) the Bible says: *"You are the God who performs miracles; you display your power among the peoples."* Additionally, in Isaiah 40:17 (NIV) the Bible says: *"See, the Sovereign Lord comes with power, and he rules with a mighty arm. See, his reward is with him, and his recompense accompanies him."* The Lord, who is Sovereign comes with power, blessings, and answers to our requests.

Prayer is a source of power God has placed in our lives with the potential to accomplish, achieve, and attain His promises. In II Peter 1: 2-4 (NKJV) reads: *"Grace and peace be multiplied to you in the knowledge of God and of Jesus our Lord, as His divine power has given to us all things that pertain to life and godliness, through the knowledge of Him who called us by glory and virtue, by which have been given to us exceedingly great and precious promises, that through these you may be partakers of the divine nature, having escaped the corruption that is in the world through lust."* God's promises reach into all areas of life. He has promised to: be with us; protect us; give us strength; answer us; provide for us; give us peace, hope and wisdom; and to always love us, just to name a few. God has given us great and precious promises, and He alone has the power to accomplish them. Pray the promises; prayer power will produce prayed promises!

In our study on prayer and promises, we have ascertained that the greatest promise of all is, God has promised to answer when we call Him or pray to Him. In Psalm 91: 14-16 (ESV): it reads: *"Because he holds fast to me in love, I will deliver him; I will protect him, because he knows my name. When he calls to me, I will answer him; I will be with him in trouble; I will rescue him and honor him. With long life I will satisfy him and show him my salvation."* Promises and prayers are deeply intertwined, in that, promises energize prayers with movement to produce answers. God answers prayer!

Another aspect of prayer potentiality is positioned in different kinds of prayers. A study of kinds of prayers would prove very beneficial to our prayer disciplines as well as prepare us to utter words of prayer needed for the circumstance or situation at hand. The Bible says in Ephesians 6:18 (NIV): *"And pray in the Spirit on all occasions with all kinds of prayers and requests. With this in mind, be alert and always keep on praying for all the Lord's people."*

Below is a list of kinds of prayers with supporting Scriptures: a few of the prayers will be expanded upon at the end of the list.

1.	Prayer of Adoration	Psalm 8:1-6, 9:1& Revelation 4:11
2.	Prayer of Agreement	Matthew 18: 18-20
3.	Prayer of Consecration	Leviticus 20: 7,8, Matthew 26: 36-39
4.	Prayer of Dedication	Psalm 19: 14, Matthew 26: 36-39, Luke 22:42
5.	Prayer of Faith	James 5:13-15, Mark 9:23
6.	Prayer of Intercession	I Timothy 2:1, John Chapter 17
7.	Prayer of Petition & Supplication	John Chapter 17 & Philippians 4:6
8.	Private Prayer	Matthew 5: 5,6
9.	Prayer of Thanksgiving	Psalm 95 & 100, I Thessalonians 5:5-19

10. Prayer of Worship   II Chronicles 16:
                          10-12, Psalm 95: 1-
                          7, Luke 11: 2-4

Of course, there are numerous prayers from the Prayer of Confession, Commitment, and Praise to the Prayer of Travailing (Warfare) and Binding and Loosing. Learning and studying different kinds of prayers will help us in developing a more effective prayer life.

The following is a review of three kinds of prayers:

A PRAYER OF ADORATION is easily intertwined with the Prayer of Worship because God is the object of both kinds of prayer. As we adore God our Father for who He is, His love for us is stirred again and our love for Him is magnified. Prayers of adoration and worship simply mean we esteem, bless, exalt, relish, dote and honor the Almighty God. It is to reflect on His character of love, mercy, grace and dominion. In Revelation 4:11 it says: *"You are worthy, O Lord, to receive glory and honor and power, for You created all things, and by Your will they exist and were created."* Hallelujah and Amen!

THE PRAYER OF FAITH is praying the will of God; it is a spoken proclamation of what the Word says. We speak it, believe it and receive it! A prayer of faith will cause us to read the Word and encourage us to trust God's Word that we have read. We can pray with an assurance when God has already made known the outcome. It is our demonstration of faith when we pray for the sick to be healed; because faith is the substance of things we hope for and the evidence of things we do not see. In James 5:15, we are told the prayer of faith will save the sick, and the Lord will raise him up. Therefore, when we pray according to this Scripture, we anticipate and expect the Word to come to fruition. However, we must pray in faith with submission when God has kept the outcome hidden. We are confident when we pray the Word of God, He will hear our prayer and He will answer our prayer.

THE PRAYER OF AGREEMENT is one of the most powerful and effective kinds of prayers we can pray and the prayer potentialities are very broad. This is a prayer that reaches beyond the normal borders of life; also, it is an utterance that brings action and answers from heaven. The Scripture states in Matthew 18:19-20 (NIV) *"Again, truly I tell you that if two of you on earth agree about anything they ask for, it will be done for them by my Father in heaven. For where two or three gather in my name, there am I with them."* The power source for this prayer is unity, harmony and oneness. When two or more are saying the same and agreeing on the same, and present it as a prayer, it moves God to action. That is tremendous!

I have adopted the Message Bible's version of Matthew 18: 18-20 as one of my life verses of Scripture: *"Take this most seriously: A yes on earth is yes in heaven; a no on earth is no in heaven. What you say to one another is eternal. I mean this. When two of you get together on anything at all on earth and make a prayer of it, my Father in heaven goes into action. And when two or three of you are together because of me, you can be sure that I'll be there."*

What makes this kind of prayer so powerful is:

1) <u>Unity</u> – the unification of two or more, oneness of thought and purpose.

2) <u>Agreement</u> –joining with another to decree and endorse the words of prayer. There is power in agreement.

3) <u>Jesus</u> – is in the midst. He is present, He will witness and agree.

4) <u>Conditions</u> – are set to bring forth movement from heaven as God goes into action.

The prayer of agreement is efficacious and compelling; whereas it is the prayer that moves God to action, and within the action are answers to our requests.

The reach of prayer potentialities is wide, deep and supernaturally power-filled. The Bible says nothing is impossible if we believe or all things are possible to those who believe. It is essential for us to believe and have faith if we are going to be recipients of blessings and promises of God. One of the Scriptures that encourages us to believe is Mark 11:24 (ESV): *"Therefore I tell you, whatever you ask in prayer, believe that you receive it, and it will be yours."* Faith must live within us to please God and trust must surge forth as we anticipate answers from God.

Yes, God is all-knowing and all-powerful, yet we are left with the responsibility to trust Him, trust His sovereignty, his power, and His Word. To trust means to rely on, lean on and be confident in the Lord. According to the Bible we can call on the Lord in our distress, and He will answer (Psalm 118:5); we trust His power to rescue (Psalm 30:3); and we trust God will save us and protect us (Psalm 91: 1-4). Trusting God is an absolute necessity. We must confidently lean and rely on the potentialities of prayer and reach of His power in prayer.

The final potentiality I will address in this chapter is the working of Holy Spirit, which is the power of the Godhead. According to Romans 8:26 & 27 Holy Spirit will help our weaknesses, impairments, human frailties and imperfections. We are thankful for the help of Holy Spirit in prayer; because often in our human frailties we do not know how to pray or what to say regarding certain situations. Nevertheless, Holy Spirit rises up within us to super-intercede for us and plead to God on our behalf and His power brings answers into fruition.

It is extremely beneficial to pray in the spirit because it builds our faith (Jude verse20) which will eradicate unbelief. When we pray in the spirit or in tongues, Holy Spirit prays through us. He, Holy Spirit enhances worship, gives spiritual edification and magnifies God. The Bible says: *"Then what am I to do? I will pray with the spirit [by the Holy Spirit that is within me] and I will pray with the mind [using words I understand];"* in I Corinthians 14:15a.*" Praying* in the spirit is prayer in our heavenly language: it is favorable to pray in tongues every day. We will experience the assistance of Holy Spirit and the activation of His power when we pray in tongues, as well as, when we decree and declare the living Word of God. Holy Spirit is our Helper!

It is paramount that we yield to Holy Spirit and embrace His help in prayer, counsel, guidance and instruction. The supernatural power of Holy Spirit moves potentialities into the realm of realities by manifesting promises, answers to our requests and blessings into our lives. It is by the manifestation of His power we also receive strength to persist in prayer and supplications. Furthermore, it is the power of Holy Spirit that gives us tenacity and empowers our faith to believe and to keep on praying. He, Holy Spirit is Counselor, He is Strengthener, He is Advocate, He is Comforter, He is Teacher, and He is Helper. He will help us Pray Until Something Happens!

CHAPTER 4

"Declare/ Decree...Praying The Word, Part I"

The living Word of God is prolific, powerful, persuasive, potent and productive. The essentiality of declaring, decreeing, proclaiming and pronouncing the Word is that God watches over His word to perform it. He alone brings His Word to fruition in our lives. In pursuit of this study on prayer, understanding the potency and significance of the written Word of God is first and foremost. Effective prayer is the living Word of God in our mouths; it is very much alive. Therefore, when we pray, we fill our prayers with the living and powerful Word of God.

The Bible is full of power; it is powerful and a living force. It is stated very well in Hebrews 4:12(AMP): *"For the word of God is living and active and full of power [making it operative, energizing, and effective]. It is sharper than any two-edged sword, penetrating as far as the division of the soul and spirit [the completeness of a person], and of both joints and marrow [the deepest parts of our nature], exposing and judging the very thoughts and intentions of the heart."* To incorporate the Scriptures into prayers and intercessions is powerful, life-changing and a guarantee for answers.

We must believe, study, trust, and obey the living Word of God. I encourage every intercessor to develop a passion for the Word, a passion so deep and pure it will drive each of us to meditate in the Word night and day as we are instructed to do in Joshua 1:8, which says: *"This Book of the Law shall not depart from your mouth, but you shall read [and meditate on] it day and night, so that you may be careful to do [everything] in accordance with all that is written in it; for then you will make your way prosperous, and then you will be successful."*

We must remain cognizant of the "if and then" principle throughout the Bible. Yes, if we meditate on the Word, chew on the Word, digest the Word, consider the Word, reflect on the Word, give the Word first place, and contemplate on the Word; then the Word will come to fruition, then we will be prosperous and successful. Also, then it will be easy and effortless to pray the living Word of God.

A renewed passion for the Word will enhance our study time and further prepare us to pray. Prayer is not power alone; it is the living word that energies and fuels the words of prayer. The Word of God in prayers and intercessions is the life-giving ammunition for the prayer; actually, the Word is the intense force of prayer. Pray the Word!

DECLARE/DECLARING

Often, we interchange the word decree and declare as if they have the same definition. Their meaning and function are different; however, when used correctly, our prayers and intercessions will be empowered and more effective.

The dictionary definition of declare is to make known or state clearly, to announce officially, to manifest, reveal especially in formal terms. Some of the Hebrew and Greek words for declare mean to recount, proclaim, announce, order or to speak out. Consequently, to declare the Word of God means to make known what is already a reality; or to acknowledge the truth about something God already revealed in His Word. Declarations acknowledge and proclaim truths about God, who He is and what He has done. For example, I declare, the Lord is my light and my salvation, whom shall I fear? I am reiterating, making it clear I have no need to fear because the Lord is my salvation, my deliverance and my rescue. I announce it into the atmosphere.

When a country declares war, they are making known the state of war now exists. When we declare in prayer, we are making known or acknowledging what God has already established as truth, hence, we are making known God's established realities. Father, I declare, "You" are my hiding place; "You" will protect me from trouble. The prayer is directed to God and the declaration is what He is and what He will do according to His written Word. Declare what God has said in His word, with the understanding God watches over His Word to perform it and He has the power to manifest His Word.

EXAMPLES OF SCRIPTURAL DECLARATIONS:

- I declare God gave me a spirit not of fear but of power and love and self-control. (2 Timothy 1:7)

- I declare I will not fear, for the Lord is with me; I declare I will not be dismayed, for He is my God, He will strengthen me and help me. He will uphold me with His righteous right hand. (Isaiah 41:10)

- The 23rd Psalm is a wonderful declaration of provision, guidance and safety. I declare the Lord is my Shepherd and provides everything I need. He leads and guides me, provides and protects me all the days of my life.

- Psalm 91 is one of most powerful declarations we can makeover and in our lives and the lives of our loved ones. I declare God is my shelter, my dwelling place, and the Shadow where I rest and I am safe. Because He is the Most High, I trust Him and do not fear.

The following Scripture, which I have referenced a number of times in Hebrews 4:12, is a dynamic declaration. I declare the Word of God is living and active, sharper than any two-edged sword, piercing to the division of soul and of spirit, of joints and of marrow, and discerning the thoughts and intentions of the heart. This is an established fact about the Word of God. When I declare it, I am announcing, acknowledging and proclaiming an established truth.

DECREE/DECREEING

The definition of decree is a formal or authoritative order, to ordain or to command. Also, it is a requirement, prescription or an allotment. Decreeing is the cause and the effect of a thing. We decree the truths of heaven to be manifested on earth so it will become a reality. For example, when a person is sick, we decree healing for them and healing is manifested. The prescription for healing is in Psalms 107:20a which says: *"He sent His Word and healed them."* Also, I Peter 2:24b says*: "By His wounds you were healed."* We decree the prescription or order for healing and the power of God will cause what He has said to manifest.

It is the order of the Lord to protect us. We can decree the Word that says the name of the Lord is a strong tower, we can run into it and be safe. Consequently, we can boldly decree Isaiah 54:17 (NKJ), which says: *"No weapon formed against you shall prosper, and every tongue which rises against you in judgment you shall condemn. This is the heritage of the servants of the* LORD, *and their righteousness is from Me, says the* LORD. *"* I decree the protection of the Lord, the formed weapon will fail.

A decree is not praying to God. It is the restating of an order or a directive already established. Moreover, it is spoken by one who has been given authority to decree, or to speak to the situation or circumstance that changes according to what has been ordained. God, by His power, brings forth the manifestation of what is decreed. Believers have the authority to decree a thing: however, God is the power that causes the manifestation. David wrote in Psalms 2:7, *"I will proclaim the decree of the Lord: He said to me, "Yes, you are my son, and today I have become your Father."* The decree is official with authority regarding the Father/Son relationship. It was the power of God that solidified the relationship or brought the decree to fruition.

It is important to command what the Word has ordained or established when praying. For example, it has been established that we are not to worry or be anxious. Therefore, my decree regarding the heavy cares of life would be: "I decree no anxiety, no stress, no worry about anything or anybody; but in everything by prayer and supplication with thanksgiving I will make my request known to God and the peace of God, which surpasses all understanding…" I decree the peace of God, I decree no anxiety, and I receive His peace, tranquility, and harmony in my life. I decree freedom from fear and receive the peace of the Lord." This is powerful! Decree it, command it, and confess it; God will perform what His Word has already established or prescribed.

The prescription or mandate from the Lord has been stated about provisions for His children. The Lord has given to us all things that pertain to life and godliness. (II Peter 1:3) We have been given all spiritual blessings, and we are to decree it so. (Ephesians 1:3) and the Lord is our Shepherd and we have everything we need. (Psalm 23:1) Decree what the Word of the Lord has ordered and ordained to be and God will bring it to fruition.

In summation, to declare means to proclaim, speak out, order or announce. Declaring when praying is to make known that which is already a reality. Also, when declaring, it is designed to announce and acknowledge truths already revealed in God's word. The Bible brings life and efficacy to the practice and process of praying.

A decree is a prescription or allotment. When we decree, we are saying as it is in heaven, so let it be on earth. Decreeing is the cause and effect of a thing. We command and speak to the situation on earth to manifest as it is in heaven as it has already been ordered. The power of the Almighty God is the vehicle of manifestation when a thing is decreed.

CHAPTER 5

"Word Hit....Praying The Word, Part II"

God's Word is persuasive, efficacious, life-changing and very much alive. The sovereign God is the keeper and performer of His Word. Pray the Word, confess the Word, put a "Word Hit" on the situation, the incident, or the circumstance and change will come. When we pray, we are to fill our prayers with the powerful, effective, and living Word of God; because God watches over His word to bring it to fruition. The guarantee for answers to prayers filled with the Word of God is in His Word. According to the Bible, God's Word will never return to Him void, empty, or unproductive. Also, the Bible states when we pray according to God's will, He will hear us and answer our request.

The Word of God is alive and full of His power and does exactly what He says. Therefore, we pray His Word confidently knowing we will be heard and answered. The process for a hit is to search and find the Scriptures that support the action that is needed for the problem, the complication, predicament, blessing, the deliverance or healing. Then, we pray the living Word; declare and decree the Word in the name of Jesus. Remember, God watches over His Word to perform it! Regardless to the mountain of trouble or trauma, negative circumstance or situation, sickness or stress, we pronounce and proclaim the Word....HIT IT WITH THE WORD. Put a "Word Hit" on it, speak what the Word says about it, for it or against it and His power will manifest the change. A "Word-Hit" will produce action, because God watches over His Word to execute it.

EXAMPLES OF "WORD HIT" SCRIPTURES:

<u>Isaiah 54:17 (AMP)</u> *"No weapon that is formed against you will succeed; and every tongue that rises against you in judgment you will condemn. This [peace, righteousness, security, and triumph over opposition] is*

the heritage of the servants of the LORD, and this is their vindication from Me," says the LORD.""

Psalm 138: 7, 8 (TPT) *"By your mighty power I can walk through any devastation and you will keep me alive, reviving me. Your power set me free from the hatred of my enemies. You keep every promise you've ever made to me! Since your love for me is constant and endless, I ask you, Lord, to finish every good thing that you've begun in me."*

Proverbs 3: 5, 6 (TPT) *"Trust in the Lord completely, and do not rely on your own opinions. With all your heart, rely on him to guide you, and he will lead you in every decision you make. Become intimate with him in whatever you do, and he will lead you wherever you go."*

Proverbs 16:3 (AMPC) *"Roll your works upon the Lord [commit and trust them wholly to Him; He will cause your thoughts to become agreeable to His will, and] so shall your plans be established and succeed."*

II Corinthians 4: 8, 9 (NIV) *"We are hard pressed on every side, but not crushed; perplexed, but not in despair; persecuted, but not abandoned; struck down, but not destroyed."*

Romans 8:31 & 37, (NIV) *"What then shall we say in response to these things? If God is for us, who can be against us? No, in all these things we are more than conquerors through him who loved us."*

I Peter 2:9 (NCV) *"You are a chosen people, royal priests, a holy nation, a people for God's own possession. You were chosen to tell about the wonderful acts of God, who called you out of darkness into his wonderful light."*

The written Word of God is a living organism and it is absolute. His Word has no failure in it and will stand forever. The Word is food for the soul and gives strength. It is a lamp and a light, and will illuminate the way we need to go. We should pulverize this Scripture, as well as meditate on it, our prayer lives will be enhanced, empowered and enlightened.

The review of the following Scripture in the next paragraph will increase our faith in regards to praying the Word of God and give us additional insight into the working ability of the living Word.

There are a number of translations of Isaiah 55:11 which warrant a close examination and additional thought. Take a moment to pulverize and meditate on each translation provided. This exercise will assist us in understanding the powerful connection between the Word and prayer.

Isaiah 55:11

New International Version

> *"So is my word that goes out from my mouth: but it will not return to me empty, but will accomplish what I desire and achieve the purpose for which I sent it."*

Whatever goes out of God's mouth will not return to Him without accomplishing its purpose.

New Century Version

> *"The same thing is true of the words I speak. They will not return to me empty. They make the things happen that I want to happen, and they succeed in doing what I send them to do."*

There is supernatural efficacy in the Word, when it is spoken, the Word makes things happen.

The Passion Translation

"So also, will be the word that I speak;
it does not return to me unfulfilled. My
word performs my purpose and fulfills
the mission I sent it out to accomplish."

God's spoken purpose and mission in His Word
will be accomplished and fulfilled.

It is significantly powerful to know God's Word
will not return void or unproductive, rather his Word
will produce the purpose for which it was sent.
Therefore, when we put a "Word Hit" on a thing, we
know unequivocally that the hit will be effective, and it
will be productive. The Amplified Bible says it very
clearly in the Scriptures we have just reviewed in Isaiah
55:11: *"so shall my word be that goes forth out of my*
mouth: it shall not return to me void [without producing
any effect, useless], but it shall accomplish that which I
please and purpose, and it shall prosper in the thing for
which I sent it." Please discern the importance of
reading, studying and memorizing Scriptures; as well
as, meditating, chewing on and digesting the living
word. Consequently, our spirit man will be equipped to
speak the Word when praying or interceding. The Holy
Spirit will bring the Word to our remembrance. And

God will perform it, manifest it or produce it. How powerful is that?

We can have faith in speaking and praying the Word because God has promised it will prosper where He sends it, the Word will be effective and never return to Him empty or unproductive. The Everyday Translation says it like this: *"The words I say do the same thing. They will not return to me empty. They make the things happen that I want to happen. They succeed in doing what I send them to do."* Pray the Word, decree the Word and it will successfully produce where and accomplish what He sends it to.

Furthermore, we must have faith and believe that God is God! He is our Father, He is the only true God, and His sovereignty should never be questioned: especially when an answer comes and it is not the answer expected. Our sovereign God always answers prayer. If God said it, that settles it! He is omnipotent....all powerful and He is omniscient....all knowing; and absolutely capable of bringing to pass what He has said. His omnipotence and sovereignty are demonstrated so marvelously in the following Scripture text in Isaiah 43:10-13 NLT: *"But you are my witnesses, O Israel!" says the LORD. "You are my servant. You have been chosen to know me, believe in me, and understand that I alone am God. There is no other God—there never has been, and there never will be. I, yes I, am the LORD, and there is no other Savior. First, I predicted your rescue, then I saved you and proclaimed it to the world. No foreign god has ever done this. You are witnesses that I am the only God,"* says the LORD. *"From eternity to eternity I am God. No one can snatch anyone out of my hand. No one can undo what I have done."*

Whatever God has said to us, whatever He has promised us in His Word, whatever the Word says about our situation or circumstance, we must have faith and believe God will bring His Word to fruition. The Word of God will stand forever; God himself declares heaven and earth will pass away, but His Word will not pass away. God will absolutely, positively watch over His word to perform it.

When praying, speak the Word of the Lord which is effective power. The Bible says in Jeremiah 1:12 NIV: *"The Lord said to me, you have seen correctly, for I am watching to see that my word is fulfilled."* Praying the word is imperative to a successful prayer life. One of the steps of prayer preparation is finding the Scripture that speaks to the situation, circumstance, problem or confession of faith. In Colossians 3:16 it reads: *"Let the word of Christ dwell in you richly, teaching and admonishing one another in all wisdom..."* Make sure the Scripture is part of the pray and have faith that God will hear you, and then be confident that He will answer your supplication.

In I John 5: 14,15 (KJ)it says*: "And this is the confidence that we have in him, that, if we ask any thing according to his will, he heareth us: And if we know that he hears us, whatsoever we ask, we know that we have the petitions that we desired of him."* We pray confidently when we pray according to the will of the Lord. God is too compassionate and full of love to hear His children's request and not answer. The NIV translation of the same Scripture reads: *"This is the confidence we have in approaching God: that if we ask anything according to his will, he hears us. And if we know that he hears us - whatever we ask - we know that we have what we asked of him."* This Scriptures causes our faith to increase knowing confidently answers will come after we have prayed. God is going to respond and answer our prayers.

Prayers, supplications and petitions should be filled with the living Word of the Lord. There is efficacy in the Scriptures; the word of God is potent, powerful and productive. Moreover, we should seek the Lord, we will find him; we are encouraged in the word to call him and he will answer. Jeremiah 29:12 says: *"Then you will call upon me and come and pray to me, and I will hear you."* Call him, he will answer, find your delight in him and He will give you the desires of your heart.

Finally, the Word says: *"When he call to me, I will answer him...."* (Psalms 91:15a) It is paramount to pray, pray without ceasing, pray in the Spirit, pray the Word and to P.U.S.H. Pray Until Something Happens!

CHAPTER 6

"When We Pray"

According to the Scriptures, we are instructed to pray without ceasing and communicate with our Father. Also, when we pray, we are to pray according to His will, then God will hear and answer us.

The following are a few "when you pray" questions:

✓ What happens when we pray, and there seems to be no answer?

✓ What are we to do when we have prayed in faith, but the answer received is not what was expected?

✓ After having prayed and received an unacceptable answer, do we question if God heard the words of the prayer?

✓ What is your query when you prayed for healing and it did not manifest?

When we pray, we recognize our state of helplessness and dependence; and it is our acceptance that God is our source, resource and supply. When we pray, it is not a means by which we try to force God's hand in our situation; rather, it is our acknowledgement of His sovereignty and our impotence. I am convinced, by the behavior of prayer alone, believers accept that God is sovereign, even though His sovereignty is not fully understood.

There is no need to and insufficient space to attempt to prove God is sovereign; however, I will refresh our memories regarding the definitions of sovereign and sovereignty. By definition sovereign means God is the supreme power and preeminent authority of His world. Also, the definition of God's sovereignty means He has the supreme authority and all things are under His control. He is King and Judge of all and has the absolute right to do all things according to His own good pleasure.

My description of God's sovereignty is He can do what He wants to, when He wants to and not at all if He does not want to. God is sovereign and He answers prayer. He is omniscient…unlimited in knowledge. He is omnipotent….infinite in power and He is omnipresent….present everywhere at the same time. God's omnipotence and sovereignty are demonstrated so marvelously in the following Scripture text in Isaiah 43:10-13 (NLT): *"But you are my witnesses, O Israel!" says the LORD. "You are my servant. You have been chosen to know me, believe in me, and understand that I alone am God. There is no other God — there never has been, and there never will be. I, yes I, am the LORD, and there is no other Savior. First, I predicted your rescue, then I saved you and proclaimed it to the world. No foreign god has ever done this. You are witnesses that I am the only God," says the LORD. "From eternity to eternity I am God. No one can snatch anyone out of my hand. No one can undo what I have done."* This is a powerful description of God our Father, with whom we have a relationship. God is the object of our prayers, supplications and petitions.

The sovereignty of God can be seen vividly in the story of Hezekiah who had received a prophetic word from the Prophet Isaiah that he was going to die. Hezekiah was totally distraught, because he had done right in the eyes of the Lord. He prayed and wept bitterly. Then the word of the LORD came to Isaiah: *"Go and tell Hezekiah, 'This is what the LORD, the God of your father David, says: I have heard your prayer and seen your tears; I will add fifteen years to your life.'* This is powerful! God heard the bitter cry and sincere prayer of Hezekiah and apparently, he had no hindrances in his life. Hezekiah PUSHED – Prayed Until Something Happened! God, in his infinite power and sovereignty, loving-kindness and mercy, heard Hezekiah's prayer and extended his life.

We were created in the image of God and to be free moral agents in His world. God divinely controls everything; however, He has given us the ability make decisions and choices. Yet in His sovereignty, God holds us responsible for our choices and life pursuits. Consequently, there is God's sovereignty and man's responsibility to consider when we pray.

We have the human responsibility to obey God's Word, which leads and guides us. In Deuteronomy chapter 10, what the Lord requires of man is stated clearly. We are to fear the Lord, walk in His ways, love and serve Him with all our heart and obey His commands. Then in Chapter 28 of Deuteronomy it states the door is open for man to choose to follow the precepts of the Lord or choose destruction. We make our choices which are judged by the sovereign God.

HINDRANCES TO ANSWERED PRAYER

Often the answers to prayers are determined by our life choices, disobedience, unsurrendered will, lack of faith and many other hindrances in our lives. It is our human responsibility to obey the Word of God in every area of life, especially in our prayer disciplines. Therefore, it is paramount to review some attributes of our humanity which are hindrances to answered prayer. The following is a list of hindrances we will review closely:

1.	Unforgiveness	Matthew 6:14, 15 Mark 11: 25, 26
2.	Releasing Offenses	Matthew 5: 23, 24, & 18: 15-17
3.	Doubting God	James 1: 5-8
4.	Lack of Faith	James 1: 6-8

5.	Wrong Motives	I Corinthians 4:19, James 4:3
6.	Unconfessed Sin	Psalm 66:18, Isaiah 59:2
7.	Neglecting God's Word	Proverbs 28:9

The following will be a closer investigation of some of the hindrances to receiving answers to prayers.

UNFORGIVENESS and RELEASING OFFENSES

It is our human responsibility to forgive and release offenses that have wounded us. The Word of the Lord says when we stand praying, forgive; moreover, we are to forgive so our Father will forgive us. When we do not forgive, we hold that person as a hostage; we are not free to receive from the Lord and neither is the other person.

An unforgiving spirit will breed and build a wall of anger, bitterness and resentment. Consequently, it will be difficult to effectively pray through that wall. We must obey the following Scripture, Matthew 18: 21,

22 which says: *"Then Peter came to Jesus and asked, "Lord, how many times shall I forgive my brother or sister who sins against me? Up to seven times?" Jesus answered, "I tell you, not seven times, but seventy-seven times."*

It is paramount for us to take action according to Matthew 18: 15-17 to resolve the problem and release the offense. The Word also encourages us to be kind to one another, tenderhearted and forgiving. Answers to prayers will not flow over an unforgiving or offended spirit; you must forgive and release offenses to receive a response to prayers offered to God.

DOUBTING GOD and LACK OF FAITH

When we pray, we must be without doubt or unbelief, and it is imperative to pray in faith. The Scripture tells us that without faith it is impossible to please God and we must believe God is our rewarder when we seek Him. Faith is trust, assurance and confidence in God, His Word and the words of prayer.

Bible says in James 1:6-8 (NCV): *"But when you ask God, you must believe and not doubt. Anyone who doubts is like a wave in the sea, blown up and down by the wind. Such doubters are thinking about two different things at the same time, and they cannot decide about anything they do. They should not think they will receive anything from the Lord."* Doubt cannot have a seat in our hearts; however, trust, confidence, reliance and love for God and His word must.

WRONG MOTIVES

When we pray, we must ask in faith, in love and with the right motive. Often a prayer with the wrong motive is selfish and always powerless. The Word tells us in James 4:3a (The Passion Translation): *"And if you ask, you won't receive it for you're asking with corrupt motives."* The Bible says if we ask and do not receive it, is because we ask wrongly. Another translation of Scriptures says wrong motive asking is done without regard for God's will. Knowing the Father's will concerning a prayer target will properly structure your prayer. If we want our prayers answered, we must be obedient and submitted to God, His will, His way and His word!

UNCONFESSED SIN

We must go before the Lord with a "clear self" and with no hidden sins or agenda. Unconfessed sins can create blockages to prayers. The Word says in Psalm 66:18 (NIV)

"If I had cherished sin in my heart, the Lord would not have listened," Confess your sins, walk in the ways of honesty and truth.

NEGLECTING GOD'S WORD

Another hindrance we must pay attention to is not hearing and heeding to the Word of God, which is unbelief and neglect. In Proverbs 28:9(NIV) it says: *"If anyone turns a deaf ear to my instruction, even their prayers are detestable."* We must not yield to unbelief; if God said it, then it is settled. Doubting God or what is written in His Word will impede our prayer progress. The Word of God is the first and final authority of all things!

We have been adopted into a royal family; therefore, we should strive to be more like our Father daily. He is holy, He is loving, He is gracious, He is forgiving and He is merciful. We cannot ignore our human frailties; neither can we ignore hindrances that would ultimately effect and affect our prayer lives. We need only to acknowledge our shortcomings and repent.

Then we can approach the throne boldly praying with up-lifted hands to God, free from anger or controversy. When we pray and pray His Word, we know confidently that God will answer. God answers every prayer!

There are a number of things to consider regarding prayers being answered to our satisfaction or not. Many have said "I prayed for healing, but it did not manifest" or "I prayed for favor for a job, but did not get the job." It is significantly important to review and understand the "if and then" principle and the human responsibility aspect of prayer. Both the principle and the aspect of prayer can be seen in II Chronicles 7:14 which reads: *"If my people who are called by my name will humble themselves, and pray and seek my face and turn from their wicked ways, then I will hear from heaven and will forgive their sin and heal their land."* It is our human responsibility to pray, seek His face, and turn from wicked ways; if we do that, then God will answer; we will hear from heaven. Also, when we pray, we must remain cognizant of the fact that God is sovereign, our relationship with him must be valid and then He will answer prayer.

The word "if" has great importance as it speaks to our human responsibility to God. Our responses to God, to His commands and to His word ultimately affect our relationship and receiving answers from Him. It is necessary to review in detail John 15; 7-10 *"If you remain in me and my words remain in you, ask whatever you wish, and it will be done for you. This is to my Father's glory, that you bear much fruit, showing yourselves to be my disciples. As the Father has loved me, so have I loved you. Now remain in my love. If you keep my commands, you will remain in my love, just as I have kept my Father's commands and remain in his love."* If we remain consistent and persistent regarding the Word of God, then, we can ask and it will be done. If we remain faithful in His love the way Jesus has remained in His Father's love, then! This is a wonderful love triangle which generates its power on the word "if."

There are many "if and then" Scriptures throughout the Bible. However, you will find almost half of the ones in the New Testament in the gospels. Jesus used "if" often when teaching his disciples putting the "if" on man and never on His Father God. Here are a few examples:

1) *"If you love me, you will keep my commandments" John 14:15 (ESV)*

2)   *"So Jesus said to her, "Did I not tell you that if you believe you would see the glory of God? John 11:40 (ESV)*

3)   *"For if you forgive others their trespasses, your heavenly Father will forgive you," Matthew 6: 14a (ESV)*

There are promises and blessings that belong to us with conditions. "If" sets the condition for our human responsibility and "then" is the result from God in response to meeting the condition. Review the following Scripture:

Proverbs 2:1-5 (ESV) *"My son, if (condition) you receive my words and treasure up my commandments with you, making your ear attentive to wisdom and incline your heart to understanding; yes, if (condition) you call out for insight and raise your voice for understanding, if (condition) you seek it like silver and search for it as for hidden treasures, then (response of meeting the condition) you will understand the fear of the LORD and find the knowledge of God."*

It would be very beneficial to study "if and then" and "if and obey" principles as we strive to improve our knowledge on prayer. The Word of God is full of foundational truths, principles and life examples that will bring edification and enlightenment to us and assist us in the development of a more effective prayer life.

CHAPTER 7

"Biblical Praying Men And Women"

There are monumental exemplifications of praying men and women in the Bible; more than I could reference in this book. However, I will examine the prayer lives of a few in this chapter because of their profound acts of fellowship, communication and communion with the Almighty God. Also, I will recap lessons to be learned and practiced; they will assist in the development of our personal prayer lives.

Biblical Praying Men and Women with Scriptural References

➤ Abraham prayed and fellowshipped with Jehovah; also, he was a participant and recipient of a covenant of greatness. Abraham was sensitive to the voice of Jehovah and obedient when given instructions and directions. He trusted Jehovah Jireh, the God who sees what things we have need of before we ask.

<u>Scripture References:</u> Genesis, Chapters 12-18.

THE LESSONS: *Prayer and fellowship with Jehovah will enhance your covenantal relationship with Him. Lean, rely and be confident that Jehovah Jireh will provide and know that obedience will position you for greatness, health and wealth.*

➤ Moses had great prayer responsibilities, wherein he prayed and communicated with Jehovah on behalf of the Israelites. He dialogued face-to-face with God, asked for their forgiveness and for His mercy. Moses was summoned four times to pray for Pharaoh and God responded. He was very devoted and connected to Jehovah through prayer, he trusted the Presence of the Lord, and he desired to know the ways of God. His reassuring message in part was: "….*My Presence will go with you and I will give you rest.*" Moses replied, "*If your Presence does not go with us, do not carry us up from here!" Jehovah replied "...I will do this thing also that you have asked, for you have found favor, loving-kindness, and mercy in My sight and I know you personally and by name." (Exodus 34: 15 – 17 Amplified)*

Scripture References: Exodus, Chapters 13-20, 25: 12-18 & 34: 1-17.

THE LESSONS: *Consistent and persistent prayer will position you for the miraculous, renew your passion for His Presence and for His Glory. Dedicated prayer time will enhance your leadership skills and clothe you with a readiness to approach the Lord. Also persistent prayer will help you walk humbly before the Lord and work effectively in His favor.*

➢ Hannah petitioned God through of her pain, tears and silent words of prayer. Hannah travailed at the altar, sometimes without audible words but in silent pain. However, God answered and granted her request. She was blessed with a son, she kept her word and dedicated him unto the Lord.

Scripture References: I Samuel 1: 6, 10, 11 & 27, & 2: 1-10.

THE LESSONS: *Pray persistently, through tears and pain, keep praying; the answer is on the way. Regardless of the hurt or the severity of the pain, be tenacious and keep praying. Pray, pray, even when there seems to be no words....keep praying, change is eminent.*

➢ Elijah was the dean of the first School of Prophets, commonly known as the praying prophet and a miracle worker. He trusted the word of Jehovah, spoke it prophetically and with no doubt. Elijah decreed there would be no rain, and God honored the word of the prophet. The prayer Elijah prayed was short, consisted of sixty-three words; however, God answered the prayer with signs and wonders on Mount Carmel, proving He was Jehovah God and Elijah was His servant. His prophecies came to fruition, he worked seven miracles and never demonstrated doubt in Jehovah Shammah, the God who was ever present.

Scripture References: I Kings Chapter 17, 18 & 19.
THE LESSONS: Pray to God and trust His Word. Do all possible to follow His directions without doubting. Pray prophetically and pray the heart of God. A consecrated lifestyle will command miracles, accompanied by signs and wonders.

➢ Nehemiah was a praying Visionary, Governor and Builder, who had a strong desire for change and restoration. His prayer life kept him focused on his endeavors and his life goal to rebuild. Regardless of the negative situations and stumbling blocks, Nehemiah remained focused on his quest.

Scripture References: Nehemiah Chapter 1, 2: 4, 5 & 4:4-14.

THE LESSONS: *Pray, pray, pray! Pray before you go, pray on the way and pray when You go, pray on the way and pray when you arrive. Nehemiah set this example for us very well. Hence he was effective in having the wall of Jerusalem rebuilt and victory over the enemy. We will have victory in our lives if we pray in advance, during and after situations and difficult circumstances we face in our lives.*

➢ David was a man after the heart of God who was, also, a prayer warrior and a praying worshipper. Regardless of what was happening in David's life, he was honest with God, a quick repenter and not a repeat offender. He worshipped and knew God as a deliverer and a way-maker. Other times he prayed to Jehovah Rohi, who was his shepherd who led him, watched over him and always gave him victory over the enemy.

<u>Scripture References</u>: 1) Prayers of Praise, Psalms 100, 113, 117; 2) Prayers of Thanksgiving, Psalms 18, 30, 32 67, 75 & 136: 3) Prayers of Confession, Psalms 6, 32 & 51; & 4) Prayers of Faith, Psalms 11, 16 & 23.

THE LESSONS: *First and foremost, earnestly seek to know the heart of God through prayer. Honesty is the best policy. Be honest with God, man and yourself about situations. Remember, God is omniscient, all knowing and He already knows your heart. Confess your sins and offenses quickly and repent. Ask for guidance and direction in prayer, then allow the Lord to bless, receive your prayers and expect answered requests. Lastly, there are many examples of prayers for a wide variety of situations in Psalms that you can pray, read, memorize, and confess as part of your prayer devotion. Become a praying worshipper!*

➢ Hezekiah was known as the praying King (Isaiah 38: 1-9), who trusted Jehovah and did that which was right in His sight (Kings 18: 3). When facing death, Hezekiah prayed and reminded God that he had walked in truth and with a perfect hearth before Him. He wept sorely; he travailed for his life.

<u>Scripture References</u>: Isaiah Chapters 36, 37 & 38: 1-7.

THE LESSONS*: Travail! Travail! I define travail as labor pain and anguish of intercession. Pray through the difficulty, pray through the pain of the unbearable, crucial and devastating circumstances. Travail and intercede through that which seems impossible. Travailing is a spiritual activity, wherein you lament, moan in anguish until you give birth to change.*

> Daniel was a righteous man of godly wisdom and spiritual intelligence. His ability to interpret dreams caused resounding notoriety among officials of the land. He proved his abilities and physical condition were enhanced by healthy eating habits; hence we have the Daniel Fast of vegetables, fruits and water whose origin is found in Daniel chapter one. He had a consistent, persistent and effective prayer life, wherein he prayed three times a day to his God even when it was against the King's order. Daniel was humble and obedient to Jehovah and a recipient of Godly favor.

Scripture References: Daniel Chapters 1 thru 6.

THE LESSONS*: Pray, pray, pray! You must pray unrelenting and persistently in faith and with no doubt. Fasting and praying should be a part of your consecration regimen because it produces humility and brings an increase in the favor of the Lord in your life.*

Trust God and His ability to deliver from any difficult and devastating situation.

➤ Anna was referred to in Scripture as a prophetess from the tribe of Asher and a consistent intercessor who devoted eighty years of her life to prayer and fasting. She prophesied of the coming of Jesus and remained in the Temple until the coming of the child Jesus.

<u>Scripture Reference</u>: Luke 2: 36-38.

THE LESSONS: *It is essential to be devoted and dedicated; and to demonstrate the discipline to pray persistently. Fasting and praying are important while awaiting answers from the Lord. We must develop a deep passion for prayer, be consistent in the assignment in anticipation of the answer....no matter how long it takes to manifest. Wait patiently on the answer to manifest.*

➤ Paul was an Apostle of Jesus, first known by his Hebrew name Saul of Tarsus. After Paul's conversion, instead of persecuting Christians, he began preaching Christianity. He was a profound instructor of prayer wherein he taught the necessity of prayer, intercession, supplication, and prayers of thanksgiving to be offered for men. Paul was a man of prayer and communed with God through prayer. The encounters during his missionary journeys and his need for triumphs demanded a persistent prayer life. Many of Paul's writings to the churches stressed the significance and preeminence of a valid prayer life, which he demonstrated throughout his lifetime. He knew the absolute necessity and power of prayer and conveyed that with an urgency to the church. Not only did he teach the people about prayer, but he prayed continually and unselfishly for them. Paul's prayers were answered; he was delivered from shipwrecks and he experienced miracles personally. He was a blessing to his followers as he taught them to pray without ceasing and to continue steadfastly in prayer.

Scripture References: They are too numerous to list, considering Paul authored 17 letters and epistles in the New Testament.

THE LESSONS: *Paul left us example after example about praying continually and consistently. We are to be disciplined, demonstrating the desire and passion for prayer and then we are to pray. If we follow the numerous examples of Paul's effective prayer life and his teachings on prayer, then we will live a life of peace, provision and protection. Also, we can be assured of a life of victory, guidance and answered prayers. The* *major lesson to be learned and practiced is being persistent and consistent in prayer, with thanksgiving.*

The following are additional lessons which are phrases from Paul's writings:

➤ *"Pray about everything and worry about nothing."*

➤ *"Pray with joy, pray in faith and pray without ceasing."*

➤ *"Devote yourself to prayer, be watchful and pray continually."*

➤ *"Also, pray earnestly day and night."*

➤ *"Prayer will give you hope, strength and encouragement."*

<u>Scripture References</u>: The phrases above were taken from Paul's writing in Romans, 1 & 2 Corinthians, Ephesians, Philippians, Colossians, and I Timothy.

It is significant to mention the countless men and women who had effective prayer lives: and their records are lessons for us; from Joshua, Samuel, Ezekiel, Job, Hosea, Zephaniah, Phoebe, Priscilla to the four gospels – Matthew, Mark, Luke, and John; and the Epistles written by Paul. We must study the lessons, read and meditate on the Scriptures and practice the examples given in each lesson.

We should follow the many examples and incorporate them into our prayer disciplines. We are in need of transformation and restoration to improve and enhance our prayer lives which will assist us in fulfilling our purposes. Therefore, let us agree to follow the examples set before us, meditate in God's word day and night observing to do His will and obey His word.

The list of praying men and women would be incomplete without Jesus, the Son of the Living God being included. Thus, I have dedicated the next chapter about Jesus, the teacher of prayer.

CHAPTER 8

"Jesus – The Teacher of Prayer"

Jesus, the Son of God and the Word made flesh, came to do His Father's will. He revealed the urgency and necessity to pray as part of the Father's will through practice. Jesus' prayer practices were phenomenal as he would rise exceedingly early to pray, and He conversed with His Father regularly. He practiced calling on His Father because He knew God would answer. We are challenged to call on the Lord; He will answer and show us great and mighty things. We are encouraged to seek the Lord with all our heart and we will find Him. This is done through prayer.

The relationship between Father and Son was intimate, and amazingly enhanced through contemplative time, communication, conversation and communion on a consistent basis. That is exactly what "prayer is" as addressed in chapter one, which Jesus demonstrated so perfectly. The disciples experienced their Master's lifestyle of prayer, meditation and contemplation, by spending time with Him and listening to His teachings. They were privy to Jesus spending quality prayer time with His Father, whom He loved, honored and obeyed. He prayed to know and remain in the will of His Father and to prevail true to His purpose and assignment.

By His prayer life, Jesus demonstrated the necessity of prayer, the importance of prayer and the urgency of prayer for everyone. There is no need to question the assignment to pray if we follow the example set by Jesus and if we adhere to His words in Luke 18:1 which says: *"And he spake a parable unto them to 'this end, that men ought always to pray, and not to faint."* There is a colloquial expression that says, 'if Jesus had to pray, what about us?' Jesus, the Son of God, our Lord and Master, Savior and Redeemer PRAYED! All mankind should pray, regardless of the title or position one might hold. We are encouraged to approach God boldly and freely with petitions and supplications and we will find help and receive answers.

In chapter three a luminous view of prayer potentialities, its reach and power were discussed broadly. Jesus allowed his disciples to experience some potentialities of prayer and power through the working of miracles, casting out demons, healing the sick and afflicted, saving the lost; and His effective prayer life.

Certainly, the Son of the Living God understood the reach of prayer, as He talked with His Father in heaven while He was here on earth. Jesus was with the Father in the very beginning of time, witnessing the Creation and the fall of man.

John 1:1-4 says: *"In the beginning was the Word, and the Word was with God, and the Word was God. He was with God in the beginning. Through him all things were made; without him nothing was made that has been made. In him was life, and that life was the light of all mankind."* It was the assignment of Jesus, the Son of God to redeem man and to reconcile us with God. Prayer and intercession were required to successfully complete His assignment.

This Scripture, in John chapter one, causes our faith to increase regarding the prayer potentialities, the reach of prayer, and prayer power simply because Jesus, God's son was intricately involved in the center of His Father's operation. The reach is deep and wide and can be understood from the teacher's words in Matthew 7:7-8 (NCV), *"Ask, and God will give to you. Search, and you will find. Knock, and the door will open for you. Yes, everyone who asks will receive. Everyone who searches will find. And everyone who knocks will have the door opened."* Jesus says in John 16:23 that the Father will give us whatever we ask for in His name. We need only to decree in the name of Jesus and declare the living word; for therein is power to receive answers when we pray.

Our personal experience of the reach of prayer was addressed in chapter four, when we were instructed to decree and declare the Word of God in prayer here on earth; and by the power of the Holy Spirit within, we will receive answers from our Father, who is in heaven. Remember, Jesus is the Word flesh-covered according to John 1:1, the Word is power-filled and powerful. When we decree the Word or make a statement of declaration from the Word, we activate the power that delivers answers to our prayers. Put a "word hit" on that difficult situation; put a "word hit" on the devastating circumstance by speaking what the Word says and anticipate answers, anticipate deliverance. Pray the

Word, it is a living organism, and God watches over His Word to bring it to pass.

The followers of Jesus had witnessed Jesus turning water into wine, perform miraculous healings, and even demonic deliverances. Yet their quest was to know and understand his prayer abilities. Because the disciples recognized His prayers were far-reaching, extremely effective and full of power, they requested a class on prayer from the teacher. This was a profound and powerful request in Luke 11: 1 (NIV): *"One day Jesus was praying in a certain place. When he finished, one of his disciples said to him, "Lord, teach us to pray, just as John taught his disciples."*

The Passion Translation refers to this popular guideline for prayer as "a model prayer" and of course, most of us know it as "The Lord's Prayer." In chapter six, the question was asked what happens "when you pray" and your answer is averse to your expectations? Studying the prayer guide of the teacher of pray will help us understand what we should say and do when we pray. Prayers are always answered.

In the model prayer, Jesus taught how to honor God, keep His name holy and ask for His kingdom to manifest His purposes in the earth. Also, He taught 1) to pray with gratefulness and be thankful for daily provisions, 2) to ask for and release forgiveness, 3) to decree protection against temptation and evil, 4) then acknowledge God who is glorious and all-powerful to answer the prayer. I suggest we use this prayer guide when we pray because it covers every area of life. Furthermore, when we pray using this guide, we avoid hindrances to answered prayer, which were outlined in chapter six.

Jesus teaches a powerful yet painful, message from His Garden of Gethsemane experience. It was the Master's desire to spend His final night with a few of His close disciples in the garden. The Scripture said Jesus was overwhelmed with sorrow and He wanted them to watch and pray one hour. The disciples were too tired and weary and fell asleep. Jesus experienced the agony of praying alone.

Jesus had prayed through many difficult situations and many traumas in His life; He always prayed in conformity to the Father's plan, purpose and will. For the first time in His life, He did not pray in conformity with the Father's will; however, he prayed a prayer of submission, a prayer of agony. In Matthew 26:39 (TPT), Jesus said with great sorrow, depression and a heavy heart: *"Then he walked a short distance away, and overcome with grief, he threw himself face down on the ground and prayed, "My Father, if there* is any way you can deliver me from this suffering,[a] please take it from me. Yet what I want is not important, for I only desire to fulfill your plan for me." Then an angel from heaven appeared to strengthen him. What we learn from this is that even in our weakest times, both spiritually and physically…. we should PRAY and submit to the will of God with the knowledge that help is nigh. We may find ourselves alone, depressed or in agony…PRAY the word, put a "word hit" on it, say what the word says and submit to the will of God.

Jesus continued praying in Matthew 26:42(NCV): "Then Jesus went away a second time and prayed, "My Father, if it is not possible for this painful thing to be taken from me, and if I must do it, I pray that what you want will be done."

Jesus, in His agony and sorrow, revealed three things in that moment: He understood the sovereignty of God, the power of a prayer of submission, and His position in the Father. The Passion Translation it reads: "Father, if you are willing, take this cup of suffering away from me. But no matter what, your will must be mine." His humble act of submission demonstrated his trust in the delivering power of His Father God.

The prayer life of Jesus teaches us the vital necessity of consistent and persistent prayer, regardless of life difficulties and challenges. Persistent prayer will help chart your course through painful negativity, disappointments, discouragements, dreadful situations and even delays. It is important to demonstrate the discipline, desire and dedication to pray regardless of the situation we are facing. We must adopt the passion for prayer that Jesus had; therein, we will habitually offer supplications and petitions to our Father, with no struggle of submitting to His will.

One of the longest prayers of Jesus is in John Chapter 17, sometimes referred to as "The Prayer of Glorification," and it is identified as a prayer of petition. By definition, the word petition means a formally drawn request that is addressed to the one in authority or power. It is a request made from something desired; it is a humble request made to one who is superior or in authority. This prayer is selfless and filled with love and concern for His Father, followers, both current and future. This prayer demonstrates Jesus' total dependence on His Father, a dependence by faith you and I must develop.

In the first petition, Jesus humbly requested that the Father glorify Him as He had glorified the Father by completing His God-given assignments in John 17: 1-

5. The additional petitions were: 2) for his disciples in verses 6-10, and 3) for the preservation and sanctification of all believers then and now in verses 11-19. 4) for "His own," the believers. The Scripture says: *"I have given them the glory that you gave me, that they may be one as we are one"* in verse 22; and 5) Jesus prayed for our union with him to emulate the union between He and His Father in verses 24-26. Jesus' petition was not for selfish gain but expressed heart concerns for his followers that He would soon leave. Furthermore, this prayer demonstrates respect for authority, relational connectivity, humility, selflessness and hope for our future.

Jesus, the teacher of prayer is the excellent example we should follow. We need to ask Him afresh "Lord, teach us to pray," teach us to communicate and commune with God, to converse with Him in fellowship as You did. Teach us facts about our assignment to pray, to call on the Lord, to seek His face, and to pray without ceasing. Reveal to us the depth of prayer potentialities, the reach of prayer and the mighty power that is activated when we pray. Lord, teach us to pray!

Instruct us again on the benefits of decreeing Your Word and making declarations from the living Word. It is your Word that You watch over to perform.

It is your Word that will never return to You unproductive, void or empty. Teach us honor and humility. Bless us when we pray to avoid hindrances to receiving answers. Increase our faith, forgive our faults, help us to confess hidden sins and strengthen us to believe. Lord, teach us to pray effectively and with love. Teach us to pray unselfishly, persistently and consistently.

Let us be faithful students in our quest to improve our prayer lives and become effective praying men and women. As we endeavor to study the lessons from our teacher of prayer, we must also make application of the same in our lives. Prayer is a gift God has given to us: it has unbelievable potentialities and unlimited power to deliver answers to our requests. Lord, teach us to pray! Teach us to P.U.S.H. – Pray Until Something Happens!

ENDNOTES

I used a variety of Bibles throughout the book. The list below is the three or four-letter codes used in the book and the version's full name or translation.

AMP - Amplified Bible

AMCPC- Amplified Bible, Classic Edition

ESV - English Standard Version

KJV - King James Version

MSG - The Message

NCV - New Century Version

NJKV - New King James Version

NLV - New Living Version

NIV - New International Version

TPT - The Passion Translation

AFTERWORD

I am extremely excited to have completed my first book. Ten years ago, the Northeast corridor of the United States experienced severe winter weather. Our area had already received large amounts of snow prior to the blizzard, known as 'Snowmageddon'on February 5th and 6th, 2010. The government, businesses, schools and churches were closed. Everything had come to a complete standstill!

What do you do when you cannot gather in the Sanctuary on Sunday morning? We had worship and the word on our telephone conference line at noon that Sunday. In an effort to not be bored, I sat at my desk in my room, to tidy up and get rid of unwanted papers. As I continued my 'busy work' a workshop booklet on prayer caught my eye. I had complied information on prayer, put it in booklet form and used it when I taught workshops and conferences. The title was "Lord Teach us to Pray" P.U.S.H. – Pray Until Something Happens. I stared at the cover sheet as if it was going to say something to me. Then suddenly deep within I said, I am going to make this a book.

On that Sunday in February and in the middle of the 'Snowmageddon', I started rewriting the information that filled twelve pages of the workshop booklet. Wow, I had started writing a book! Actually, a few months prior to winter setting in, I had started writing another book on a totally different subject from one of my sermons. However, after writing a chapter or two, I quickly ran out of steam and did not have enough motivation to write consistently. I realized that Sunday, I now had two books started in my computer, just waiting for me to write.

In March 2020, I found myself shut-in due to the Corona Pandemic. I made a commitment to write and complete the book on prayer. I conceived this book 'Snowmageddon' and now ten years later I have given birth to the book during the shut-in of the Corona Pandemic. What an awesome time for its release!

This is a powerful and prophetic season for my book on prayer titled, **Lord, Teach Us To Push....Pray Until Something Happens!** to be published. Considering the state of our world, our country, the devastation caused by Covid19 and the many alterations we have had to make in our lives, our need for prayer is first and foremost. I am certain beyond any doubt, this book has taught you the what, the when, the why and the how about prayer. Also, I am positive you have learned the potentialities of pray and the power of putting a word hit on a situation. Absolutely, I believe your prayer regiment and prayer disciplines have been enhanced after reading this book.

I am extremely elated I fulfilled a ten year aspiration with the profound help of my writing coach and Holy Spirit: I did not quit and I never gave up. I had received a number of prophecies on different occasions about writing books. One prophet said he saw multiple books within me and I needed to write, write, and write.

I am excited and thankful to see this prophetic word come to fruition in my life. The very first book I started about eleven years ago will be book number two and I am currently writing it. While writing this book on prayer, I have received titles for two additional books that I intend write. And to God be the Glory!

This is amazing, watching my dreams, desires, and aspirations come true. I encourage you to be faithful to the purposes God has selected for you to do. Always follow His lead and never give up. I am fulfilling my purpose as a 'teacher of teachers' and a prophetic leader in the Body of Christ. It will be done through books I will author within the next year.

I live and practice the prayer principles within these pages and I know for certain, the information you have read has absolutely blessed your life. And to God be the Glory!

BIOGRAPHY

Bishop Carrie J. Surratt is Senior Pastor of The Lord's Church of Restoration in Clinton, Maryland, and Founder and President of Bible Prayer Time Faith Ministries, Incorporated. Bishop Surratt is the Academic Dean of the Restoration Development Institute. She serves on the College of Bishops and the Bishops' Council of Kingdom Fellowship Covenant Ministry (KFCM) of Baltimore, Maryland. Also, her assignments with KFCM is Bishop of Intercessory Prayer.

Bishop Surratt is a native of Alexandria, Virginia, where she completed her primary education. She pursued her academic studies at George Washington University, Washington, DC; University of Maryland, College Park; Washington Bible College, Lanham, MD;

and Rhema Bible School. Bishop Surratt earned her Master's Degree in Religious Studies at Washington Saturday College. She received an Honorary Doctorate of Humane Letters from Washington Saturday College, Washington, DC. In November 2015, Bishop Surratt received an Honorary Doctorate of Ministry from Kingdom Covenant Theological Bible College, Baltimore, MD.

Bishop Surratt has served on the planning committee for Minority Women in Ministry for the National Council of Churches, USA. She was selected and is profiled in "Women of Achievement," the first book of history in Prince George's County, Maryland, that chronicles women and their accomplishments.

By due prudence and examination, Bishop Surratt was consecrated into the Episcopacy by the Sacred College of Bishops in 2001. She was further elevated in the Episcopacy in November 2004 and is the Presiding Bishop of Restoration Covenant Ministries (RCM) of Clinton, MD. Restoration Covenant Ministries is the apostolic and spiritual covering for businesses, pastors, and para-churches and para-ministries.

Bishop Surratt attended The Joint College of African-American Pentecostal Bishops' Congress in

Cleveland, Ohio, in 1998 and was one of only three females' bishops in attendance. She has been an active member for twenty (20) years; and served as Secretary for the Advisory Board for 10 years. She is also affiliated with Boundless Ministries, Inc. in District Heights, Maryland. She has also served in missions preaching, teaching, distributing food, clothes, and medicated sleeping nets to Kenya and Uganda, East Africa.

Bishop Surratt is an anointed preacher, a profound teacher of the Word of God, and an excellent conference speaker. Her greatest desires are to win the lost, bring restoration to fallen humanity, and be an effective servant to the Body of Christ for God's glory.

www.ingramcontent.com/pod-product-compliance
Lightning Source LLC
Chambersburg PA
CBHW060551100426
42742CB00013B/2521